BASED ON A TRUE JOURNEY

GRACETHROUGH

Again

TIANA SANDERS

FOREWORD BY DR. JEREMIAH DANIEL DAVIS

Book Cover Design Concept: Tiana Sanders
Book Cover Design Illustration: Q11 Studios

Printed by Prize Publishing House, LLC in the United States of America.

First printing edition 2024.

Prize Publishing House
P.O. Box 9856, Chesapeake, VA 23321
www.PrizePublishingHouse.com

Library of Congress Control Number: 2023921182

ISBN (Paperback): 979-8-9892479-4-3
ISBN (E-Book): 979-8-9892479-5-0

DEDICATION

I dedicate this book to anyone who has acknowledged and nurtured the best in me, even when I presented the worst.

"There is no greater agony than bearing an untold story inside you."

-Maya Angelou

CONTENTS

FOREWORD

In the pages that follow, you will embark on a transformative journey guided by the remarkable wisdom of Tiana Sanders in her book *GraceThrough Again*. With grace as its compass, this book is a testament to the indomitable human spirit and the profound capacity we possess to overcome life's most challenging trials.

Tiana Sanders' words resonate with the authenticity of someone who has faced adversity head-on with unwavering courage and resilience. Her story is one of unwritten chapters, where the turning of each page reveals a powerful narrative of fortitude and inner strength.

As you delve into these pages, you will discover the essence of grace in the most unlikely of places, in the darkest corners of life, and in the face of seemingly insurmountable obstacles. Tiana's journey reminds us that grace isn't just a state of being; it's a force that can reshape our destinies and empower us to rise above any circumstance.

GraceThrough Again serves as a guide, an inspiration, and a testament to mankind's ability to overcome, adapt, and emerge stronger. Tiana's story is a beacon of hope, illuminating the path for those seeking resilience in their own lives.

As one who has the honor to pastor this brilliant mind, I've watched this skillful essence own her past, present, and future with integrity and honesty, all while refusing to be afraid to accept her part in the failure and success of her narrative.

This book is a celebration of the human capacity for grace, a testament to the boundless potential for overcoming, and a reminder that fortitude is a strength that resides within us all. It is with great pleasure and anticipation that I invite you to join us on this transformative journey through the pages of *GraceThrough Again*.

~Dr. Jeremiah Daniel Davis

INTRODUCTION

If you're reading this book, it might be driven by a desire to support the author, fueled by curiosity, or simply the pursuit of an engaging read. Whatever the reason, welcome! I trust that something within these pages will serve as a reminder that your life story holds significant value. The narrator of your existence, your Creator, certainly believed so, and that's why you're still standing.

Within the upcoming pages, I've recounted moments from my life's journey thus far. Some chapters remain unwritten and not yet ready for public viewing. Some stories are still in the process of unfolding but are worth sharing for both your understanding and mine.

As a business owner, I established Grace Space Boutique as a means of expressing my desire to present a better image in the face of adversity. As cliche as it sounds, during challenging times, we really don't have to look like what we go through. Now, as an author, I aim to convey the message that we become better when we place our trust in God to guide us through challenges with grace. While the term "GraceThrough" may not be found in any dictionary, it has provided some definition for some of my life's experiences so far. The word "Again" can be broken down as A-gain, meaning that even a loss can mean a gain in your journey.

As you read through the contents of this book, I invite you to think about the following questions:

- Where does your relationship with God fit into your life's journey?
- How do you navigate challenging situations, and what lessons are you learning or need to learn?
- What words do you employ to describe your life?
- How do others perceive you, and do their descriptions hold significance for you?
- Have you successfully broken free from unhealthy cycles?

- Can you recognize the beauty within the most challenging circumstances?
- What are you holding on to that has already moved on from you?
- Which spaces in your life are you gracing?

This book represents a compilation of events, excerpts from letters, insights, and encounters that contributed to shaping my inner self as I have journeyed through life. I also share some acronyms, a way that God has spoken to me through words. Life is far from simple, yet challenging circumstances aren't necessarily a bad thing. This book has been therapeutic for me. I really hope it helps you too.

1

GRACE THE SPACE

GraceThrough

GraceThrough is a concept derived from the word "breakthrough," a term this book will use to describe the beauty found in triumphing over adversity, overcoming challenges, shattering recurring patterns, gaining wisdom, and becoming who God called you to be, gracefully. It is also used to describe what we bring with us on our journey to better. GraceThrough is my testimony. I grew up in church and was what some would call a "good girl." While I am grateful for my upbringing, it did not exempt me from the consequences of bad decisions or life's challenges. The good girl experienced some "bad," but there was an undeniable grace on my life that I did not always see, which got me through life over and over again.

The intentional use of "again" in the title *GraceThrough Again* emphasizes that every challenge we face plays a role in our growth, even if we don't recognize it right away.

Pause and consider -you've faced difficulties and enjoyed successes in the past, and you can do it once more— where it is A-gain! Even your loss does not have to be a loss. It can serve as a platform for wisdom, knowledge, and understanding that you did not have before. Now that is GraceThrough.

GraceThrough, as a phrase, speaks to your journey and arrival at your destined appointments. Often, when you have an appointment with a doctor, dentist, or even in business, as a courtesy, you're sent a reminder of the date and time. Let this be a reminder that you have

somewhere to be! Hardships, tests, battles, or procrastination can't stop you from getting there unless you
allow it.

Sometimes, you live because that's what you are supposed to do. Now live because it's what you're born
to do. God has a plan for your life! The word grace
incites feelings of beauty, class, and style. However, we
all know some spaces that can be funny-looking and
downright ugly. Even the unattractive moments have
purpose and beauty.

Ultimately, the key lesson is that without a battle, where
is the win? The battle often is against our own will,
desires, and decisions, not just people. Sometimes, all
it takes is a shift in perspective in battle. In my life, I've
weathered periods of homelessness and relished moments of luxurious living. I've experienced both healing
and illness, periods of despair and seasons filled with
unspeakable joy. I've been lost, and I have been found.
What transpired between these moments is what truly
defines GraceThrough.

GraceThrough encapsulates the abundance of God's grace I've received in my life. It also reflects the grace I've been able to extend even in battle. Life is bound to present its fair share of trials, yet what truly counts is how we navigate through them. My hope is that this book will encourage you to consider what you're carrying with you as you break through and GraceThrough life. Everything you face presents an opportunity for you to add or exchange something that will bring you closer to uncovering your identity as a child of God. Don't you dare enter another test, situation, season, or event without pulling out the lesson, blessing, or virtue that you need. If you do not retrieve or learn through what you go through, you will find yourself in a loop of transition that you were never meant to be in. I am continually discovering that life's challenges are not meant to stop our progress (unless it's a rebuke to stop us from growing in the wrong direction) but can actually nourish us. With time, you will even find gratitude for the trials you face because they can be used to make you better. Even your naivety and ignorance can birth a lesson.

For example, I had to take charge of my emotional spending habits when I declared bankruptcy at twenty-five years old. The main reason was a car repossession. While it was a lot to take in, I eventually had to question whether the repossession of my first car was a spiritual attack or simply a consequence of my poor spending choices. I knew the car note was due each week (first mistake). However, my home needed new pillows, silk flowers, and portraits. I thought the car payment could wait. The power of GraceThrough showed me that yes, I needed to budget and be responsible, but I also needed to deal with the need for all of the "nice things."

All of the nice things wouldn't abandon me like some of the nice people did in my life. I was able to leave them there, and they would be in the same place I had left them. I could surround myself with beauty even though what I may have been facing at the time was ugly. See, that too is a part of GraceThrough, uncovering motives for our unhealthy or questionable habits. Now that my motive was uncovered, better decisions followed. I'll be able to genuinely enjoy the blessings of the Lord in the houses and cars that I will have and be a blessing to others with. Gracethrough to better decisions is a sure-fire way to grace your space, but first you have to show up to get there.

CHAPTER

2

GRACING THE SPACE
Show Up!

The art of showing up is an important part of GraceThrough. The sum of Gracethrough is what happens between where you are and where you need to be. The biggest part of the equation is, you. We will call you being present, "Gracing the Space." Gracing the space speaks to showing up and shining your light in places that have no light or have dim lights and assisting fellow lights in shining. Sounds graceful, doesn't it? It can actually feel like the opposite. There will be spaces where your light is not understood. There will be times when it is rejected. Show up anyway. Let's be clear: the light we're referring to is not to bring glory to yourself. Any honor you receive is a byproduct of God's light. The scripture that comes to mind when thinking about gracing a space is Matthew 1:16, "Let your light so shine before men, that they may see your good works, and glorify your Father which is in heaven." It will not be welcomed or understood by everyone. Don't get tripped up on that. I have been stuck in rejection to the point that my entire life was stagnant. Let this be the push you need to move on. Let's keep reading.

In my life, I've written so many random letters to a younger or current version of myself. I would sometimes go back and read them and surprise myself. Unfortunately, many of my diaries, which housed some of my juiciest and intimate thoughts, were lost. I started to believe that someone found them and turned them into movies. You'd be surprised if I told you which movies. In any event, I cannot remember life before third grade for some reason. What I do remember was being such a stressed-out child. Unfortunately, the stress ripped me of joyous memories until I'm around family and friends who make me remember the good times. Many of the letters provide prompts to help me to remember. I'll share some of those, too. I'm grateful for the times I was talking to myself. Don't let anyone tell you that a little bit of talking to yourself is unhealthy. When you start talking back, you might need to talk to someone else.

One of the letters I wrote to myself came after I was having a conversation with someone who reminded me of all the things that I had been through and accomplished. She was so proud, but as she spoke, my heart began to break. While it was commendable that God graced me in such an amazing way, I grieved for the unmatured Tiana, who made the best of what she knew and had. I experienced breakthrough so much in life, but I never really stopped and graced my own space.

The letter started like this:

> *"I want you to know that there was no amount of money, time, or energy that you could have given to stop them from leaving*

you. The truth is every person and thing that you lost was protecting you. I know at times, you settled and went above and beyond, hoping that someone would see your value. But in times when you had nothing to give or anything left for a performance, it was God's perfect love that stayed and never left you. The cold and lonely nights, couch surfing, and wondering if anyone loved you will not be your final destination. They are moments that will be distant memories. As you continue to live, you will realize just how loved and valuable you are by your Heavenly Father before anyone else. You've been blessed with great relationships and a resiliency to bounce back from anything life has thrown at you. I wish you did not have the burdens of life so heavy on you in your youth, but I promise you it will get better."

Life did get better. Life will be better. GraceThrough surely happened before the term was created. In hindsight, I was fighting to improve the quality of my life in much of what I was doing. Sometimes, GraceThrough is waking up and being intentional about not being the worst version of yourself. For me, that meant vision board parties, adult sleepovers, self-care activities, girl groups, and even letters like the one you just read. Even the lightest of moments turned into snot-nosed lamenting and self-reflection, not just for me but for others who were there too. There were so many moments that even my brokenness fostered environments of change; even when I didn't know it, all I had to do was show up. I realize there was always an attack to prevent me from just showing up, even from an early age. That is where "Grace the Space" began to form. It was clear that I had to show up, but that did not mean it would be easy to do so.

I identified barriers in my life that stopped me from getting to places where I needed or desired to be even early on in life. At some point those barriers became blessings because they taught me boundaries, making it safer for me to get to the spaces I needed to grace even if it was a struggle to get there.

I remember hospital and emergency room visits as a child, that tried to stop me from showing up. I had a severe mental health crisis in middle school that took me out of one of my favorite places to be, school. It all began with severe headaches and a change in my patterns leading me to visit the doctor. I was asked so many questions about what was going on with me but I had no answers. The doctors didn't either other than suggesting I see a psychologist. I vividly recall a moment when I found myself sitting on the floor, rocking back and forth, hearing the voices of my family, yet unable to comprehend their words. It was like I was a walking zombie with limited words or desire to do anything. I had this pounding in my head that would not go away. I remember settling in my mind that I would need to figure out how to live with it so that I could get back to my normal schedule. During this period, I refused to eat, avoided showering, and was just blank. I attempted to speak but found myself unable to articulate. This alarmed my family, particularly my siblings, who watched everything unfold.

As the eldest child in our home, I took pride in being a big sister, daughter and a student who did well academically. I never missed school, snagged many academic awards, and was considered smart by those I encountered. However, during this challenging time, not even my giftedness or good-girl nature could carry me through. I literally felt like I was losing my mind. I know it was out of concern, but it seemed as if even my family was frustrated with me, I don't know how I could show up in this situation, but I know who did, God.

Despite attending church weekly as an escape from home, I didn't acknowledge God as my healer yet. Although still very much "off" I went to church and sat there as blank as I could be. My mother alarmed the leaders of what was going on with me in hopes someone would pray for me. That Sunday I was escorted to the children's room in the back of the church where the ministers, including my grandmother, began to pray for me. Due to my difficulty in speaking and overall weakness, my participation was kind of limited at first. I wasn't expecting much-but remember everyone surrounding me as I just stood there, detached from the reality of that moment. Boy oh boy did they pray. At first, I just watched and then they began to call on Jesus, together. Eventually, tears welled up, and something within me began to break free. My body responded in a way it hadn't in a long time. I was clapping, crying, and smiling. I witnessed and experienced the beauty of God's love, taking control and providing what I couldn't achieve on my own or with a physician. I showed up to church and left with an appreciation for God as a healer that will forever remain etched in my memory.

GraceThrough To Exchange

The heaviness of what I faced then was real. The heaviness of life in general can be the same. I will challenge you in this moment: whatever your vice is, take that away for this moment. Whoever your person is, dismiss them from the equation for right now. Anything that is temporarily lifting that heaviness, take it away for a minute and breathe. If that is hard to do, it will be hard to grace a space. There is something that you need and that I needed to really begin to show up in my own life.

That something is giving your will and way over to God and allowing Him to grace you with what you need to continue the path He has prepared for you. Another Bible scripture that comes to mind is found in Matthew 11:28-30, "Come unto me all ye that labor and are heavy laden, and I will give you rest. Take my yoke upon you, and learn of me, for I am meek and lowly in heart, and you shall find rest unto your souls. For my yoke is easy, and my burden is light."

Gracing a space happens after you've had an exchange with your Heavenly Father. That exchange allows you to free yourself of the natural burdens of this world as you live, learn, and mature in your God-given life. Life can be *all the things* you don't want, but it doesn't have to be. What if the very thing that's holding you back can not only free you but help liberate someone else? What if what you're stressing right now will provide a pillar of peace in the midst of chaos?

Grace the Space

"Grace the space" can be a tricky phrase. In essence, it's saying you must find the grace needed to show up, but for that to happen, you must first show up. My first-time entertaining counseling, I thought I really was showing up. I was so proud of the fact that I sought healing on someone's couch. I poured out everything I wasn't ashamed of saying. I was then told the hurt was not my fault but was my responsibility to heal from. I thought it was the most ridiculous and insensitive thing to say after I had revealed some of my most shallow, intimate secrets. The audacity of this stranger to suggest that I had not been trying to heal! Why did they think I was in their office, not being completely honest in the first place? I did not really show up; my public representative, who was not ready to heal, was on that couch.

Perhaps what brought me to counseling was louder than the voice of the therapist. Needless to say, I didn't go back, but I later heard the same sentiments in another form. This time, it went something like, "Girl, build a bridge and get over it." I showed up for that because I was ready to grace the space of healing. When all of me showed up, I could better receive the instruction.

Finding grace in spaces of life requires your presence, all of you. As a delivered people pleaser, showing up wasn't the hard part for me. Let's park here for a moment. A people pleaser usually considers everyone else before themselves or makes pleasing others a priority. If you struggle with that type of personality, dig into why you are that way. It may be rooted in something else. Then we have a selective people pleaser. This type has the urge to please only certain people for a certain reason. You may actually dismiss others who you don't deem important enough. This can speak to your character more than some of the rooted issues in people pleasing. Whatever the case may be, it can make you show up with the wrong motive. Stay home (figuratively speaking) until you can deal with your desire to please people.

Your presence plays a major role in any space you enter, but the key lies in the essence of your presence. How and why you show up matters. If you present yourself as a vulnerable target for negativity, consider the impact you're making. Showing up solely to absorb external influences may likely result in a sense of emptiness. Conversely, arriving with an inflated sense of self leaves little room for the beauty of a graceful exchange with people and, most importantly, your Creator. Stay conscious of being rooted in grace, ensuring it comes from a genuine and humble place rather than a prideful one. Prioritize cultivating the best version of yourself before extending your best to others. Consider your motive for gracing the spaces you are in.

I can recall a time when I had become so driven by the opinions others held of me that I felt compelled to be present, absorbing both positive and negative feedback, regardless of its nature. An incident occurred during my time at a job where I was not shielded from the impact of a traumatic event involving a client. The appropriate course of action would have been to resign on that very day. However, I was determined to ensure that, despite fearing for my safety, I showed my dedication to completing my tasks and handling the incident for the greater benefit of the company. Unfortunately, the way I mishandled the grace to show up was detrimental to my mental well-being. I showed up expecting empty spaces to fill me up. Neither my co-workers nor the company had the capacity to give what was needed when I showed up. After making the hard decision to leave that place of employment, it pushed me to show up not just for others but more importantly in that moment for myself.

The time that I had off before going to the next place of employment taught me about the space of time. Working a full-time job is a commitment that should not be taken lightly. Think about it, you spend much of your time, energy, and creativity within those eight or more hours a day. That is a space all on its own. A space that can push you to grow or pull you to stagnation. During the next phase my life, I can see that those I spent that much time with would have to encourage me to Grace the Space to show up. Because the tests of life that were coming would try to get me to retreat, but no matter what, I had to show up. Those around you will play an important role in you getting to where you need to be so, choose wisely.

Everyone should have measurements and boundaries regarding people, situations, and their space. The spaces that you're not welcomed to or invited to are not the spaces you should concern yourself with gracing. Now, can you grace those spaces too? Maybe so. There is no way we can discuss gracing a space and not acknowledge spaces that are not deserving of what you carry. If you ever find yourself in any of these situations, grace the space of goodbye:

- Any space that does not appreciate or acknowledge your value or causes you to devalue yourself
- Spaces of extreme chaos and or confusion
- Spaces that have rejected God profusely
- Spaces that drain without the opportunity of replenishment
- Spaces of extreme darkness that you are not led to shed light in
- Spaces or places you were delivered from not to return again
- Spaces that rely on the worst version of you
- Spaces that can destroy your destiny
- Spaces without any boundaries or limits

- Unbalanced spaces that lead to darkness
- Any space that is harmful without reprieve or healing

One of the most challenging circumstances to navigate is the act of clinging to something that has already released its grip on you. Sometimes, this occurs because you're unaware of the detachment, and other times, the hope of reconnecting drives you. These are spaces marked by rejection, and regardless of your perspective, they're spaces that fail to embrace who you really are.

Just as you have your boundaries, there are spaces you should not entertain in your life. Examine your situation through the lens of healing and wholeness and determine when it's appropriate to bid farewell to such spaces. You might be investing time, energy, money, and resources into something that has essentially shut you out. What might this look like? Here are a few examples:

- Persisting in a job that undervalues you or where your time has run its course.

- Remaining committed to an uncommitted partner.

- Seeking validation from individuals not meant to provide meaningful insights into your life, simply because you crave their acceptance.

- Excessively accommodating individuals who offer nothing in return.

- Entertaining those who operate in false humility (when pride is disguised to appear humble).

- Staying in imbalanced or unequal relationships to avoid loneliness.

These are just a few instances, but the underlying point is clear. Spaces that fail to enhance your sense of worth in God or diminish your value are not worth your time and energy. While these spaces may warrant your prayers, they do not demand your physical presence. Always remember that your space should be treated in a way that respects your genuine worth, without ever being subjected to your flaws and shortcomings, even if you might personally believe you are damaged.

CHAPTER

3

DAMAGED GOODS
Grace Through the Label

Damage does not disqualify you from your divine destiny. With every break and bruise, you may feel less and less valuable, but you're not. Some damage is more pronounced than others. That can sometimes mean the healing is also greater. I struggled to share some damage because I did not want to acknowledge how much it impacted me. During one of the hardest years of my life, I experienced heartbreak, failure, loss of two loved ones, wayward friendships, and a sickness that almost took my life in less than nine months. That period in my life required a connection to my Creator for living that I honestly did not have. On top of that, the pinnacle of my damage in the same year was a divorce. A divorce that separated me from the relationship that would have helped me get through the other hard times but left me feeling even more damaged. In those nine months, I carried the weight of shame, sickness, and isolation because I yielded my authority to it rather than posturing myself for victory over it. However, I GracedThrough before and had to find the resolve that I would, again. Although I carried the weight of the world, during those nine months, I refused to give birth to it.

Although uncomfortable, those times highlighted the damage I felt from previous times that I did not properly GraceThrough. Like the night I experienced the damage of sexual violation. I slept in a fetal position for the entire night. I convinced myself it was my fault and that because I let him in my home and flirted with the idea that night, it was okay. But it wasn't. By taking responsibility for the person who violated me, I internalized the damage for both of us. The label not only affected how I viewed myself but also how I permitted others to devalue me. I thought less of myself based on what I had allowed, making me feel like damaged goods from within. This internal label acted as a signal for those who sought to exploit the damage. I found myself using the violation as a parameter for how much I was willing to take from those who expressed romantic interest in me. It was not a matter of value more than it was about tolerance. The damage used to describe what I felt indirectly began to define parts of me that were not as damaged. My self-esteem and worth in which were usually not in-question became the topic for discussion and compromise. Being damaged is a decision we can't afford to make.

Have you ever gone through something and believed that, based on your circumstance, your level of value decreased? It could have been a loss of any kind, sexual assault, an embarrassing event, or just a change in your esteem. As a result, you feel your usefulness, significance, or desirability is lower than it should be, and your damage justifies it.

You may not have expressed verbatim that your value decreased, but you position yourself to receive what's best for everyone but you. This can look like hyper-focusing on others' success more than your own, settling in areas and justifying it through the imbalance of your self-worth, or forgiving and restoring based on emotion and not principle. If you're not careful, you will be engulfed with a life that reflects the pain of your damage more than the grace to overcome it.

This was a space I occupied very well. I wore the damaged goods label as a badge of honor. I was still good, even though I was damaged. God was still good even though I was damaged. The thing about the truth is it doesn't need an "even though," so why do we? When you label yourself, you section off the spaces of life that don't accept that label. If I am damaged goods, how likely am I to grace a space called perfection? (James 1:4) If I am damaged due to unhealed rejection or trauma, am I truly embracing people, places, and things outside of that damage, or am I living the label?

This became very relevant to me amid the divorce. Truthfully, I did not want it. I said yes with my mouth, but my heart begged for it all to change. Even though the marriage was not fruitful at that point the label of rejection told me otherwise. I wanted the circumstances surrounding the divorce to change more than what needed changing in me. I remember saying things like "we did things right, why is this happening" or standing on the fact that I was fighting for my marriage! Or was I? See, living the label of rejection and damage will make you hold on to things that let you go. I carried this trait in other spaces of my life too. My cut off game was not strong, at all. It led me to try to prove to people who expressed they did not want me and all that I could bring that, in fact, they did. If the job undervalued me, I would put in more work. If someone suggested I wasn't qualified. Back to school, I would go. Were you sick of me? Be healed with me. Oh, so I don't fit in? Guys, look at what I can do!

The label went from rejection to doormat very quickly. The damage not only labeled me but gave me meaning. How was that good? It wasn't good to be damaged, and the label actually did more damage than good. You see, how you can play on those words? That's what we do in real life. We convince ourselves that if there is a glimmer of good, it's good. At some point, my standards began to disappear when I'd say things like, "At least he doesn't treat me like so and so....." Even the bare minimum can be justified for those who label themselves damaged goods. I found myself in situations that you wouldn't believe! I was even more damaged than before. The thing about a standard is it keeps out unwanted things, but once your damage lowers that standard, hold on tight for the things you will let in. Accepting less will not get you more. The label of being a damaged goods limits how you GraceThrough. You can't GraceThrough or get through something that you have made a permanent fixture in your life. If you succumb to the damaged goods label, you've positioned damaged goods as a principle you live by rather than grounds for GraceThrough.

I remember one day when I was staying with someone after I had become damaged goods because I was homeless. I came home later than normal. All the lights were off, the doors were closed, and my phone was dead. I knocked on the door for almost an hour to no avail. The house was shut down, and everyone in it was asleep. I had no money or transportation to go anywhere else, and I was mentally and physically exhausted from whatever I did that day. It was freezing. I looked around on the porch, grabbed whatever clothing items I could find, and created a pallet on the floor, and I cried myself to sleep.

I convinced myself I deserved to sleep there that night because I should have come back earlier (damaged goods principle). After all, they were doing me a favor by allowing me to stay there. I appreciated the grace in that moment to get through that night. However, I needed to activate GraceThrough to get me through that lifestyle. The lifestyle in which your decisions and circumstances reflect the damage you feel.

Sometimes, we convince ourselves that our present circumstance disqualifies us from what is good or God's best for us. Was it God's will for me to sleep on the floor in the freezing cold to prove that He is good? Probably not. Did I deserve to sleep on the floor because I did not have a home? No. Was it sad? Yes. As damaged goods, it could have pushed me to lash out. After all, I was already damaged. What did I have to lose? Actually, a lot. So do you. Before you lash out again at what you deem unfair, consider what you have to lose or what you will forfeit to gain. As sad as that situation seemed, it was an opportunity to experience newness in my thought patterns concerning not only my living arrangements but a shift in my life. I began operating in spaces where damaged goods did not belong - in newness. I declared it would be the last time I would be put in a situation like that - it was the beginning of me gracing through poverty, even in my mindset.

I did not have all the money I needed for everything the newness presented. However, I had a principle that worked. If I gave God back what He gave me, it multiplied and was sustained. I was so excited at any chance to give or help others as an act of gratitude, and I knew that it was helping me establish the beginning of the rest of my life as it related to poverty. Some relationships disappeared, and I was told I was acting funny when I began to change. It was not something I needed to consume myself with because who and what was meant for me would understand or at least not pull me away from the progress I was trying to make.

As you GraceThrough to progress be mindful of the beginning stages of anything in your life. There are often attacks early on during transitions to get you to stop growing past the damage so that you will never get to greater. You take extra special care of people/things early on in hopes that they will grow healthy and strong or stay like new. You should put that same attention into your newer self as you break free of what held you back. If there is anything that stands in the way of your newness, such as people, places, and things that were attached to you in your damaged season, keep going, and as you heal, they will fall off or begin to heal too.

I was in a testimony service one night, and the person telling their testimony had a stroke. There were still some physical signs of the stroke, but she declared healing even though her body said something else. This was a new posture that she had to maintain because her physical body was impaired. What stood out to me was her stating that if the side effects of the stroke were still on her, they, too, would have to praise the Lord. It spoke volumes to me. Not even the things that are meant to stop us can prevent us from GraceThrough. She has since been healed with no physical trace of the stroke. That was a prime example of growing past the damage. A true commitment to your GraceThrough says even the traces of trauma will glorify God.

I want to make sure I can acknowledge some things that happened to you seemed unfair, unjust, or made you feel unloved. That does not change the fact that God's essence is fair, just, and loving. This life can leave you feeling stuck in a temporary moment. Perhaps it's time to break through your thoughts to the grace found in God's thoughts toward you. Let the depth of your damage drown in God's plan for your life.

Declaring that you are damaged goods suggests that based on what has impacted you, not even what God says about you can change it. Can I share a secret with you? You are not as damaged as you think, your pain can actually sharpen you in amazing ways.

Part of the issue may be that you have not acknowledged that you've gone through things and have been successful in the past. Whether it is similar or a different battle, you are and have been an overcomer. Bring all that with you as you GraceThrough whatever you're facing or will face. Consider if you're still operating as the expired version of yourself. For example, the old you may have been a bit of a people pleaser; the new you may realize you don't even like people that much. You love them, but you find solace in your own company at times. If that didn't hit close to home, maybe the old version of you was content walking around being mean because it's who you are or where you came from, but then you discovered the art and beauty of kindness and genuine exchange. In consideration of the new you, it's time to fix your expired face. Okay, maybe that one did not apply. Perhaps the old you had no problem being all things to all people until you realized you were empty. While America may run on a particular coffee and donut brand, you do not. It's time for the new you to ensure your safety before anyone else's.

I digress in hopes that the point was made. Even the "that's just who I am" type of person changes. You don't have to be loyal to the version of yourself that didn't go through what you went through. Give yourself some grace for still being here and not giving up even when you could have. God knew your mistakes, messes, and milestones and ordained you to be here in this very moment. Damaged? No. Destined? Yes.

There is something I would like to revisit from what was said a few paragraphs ago. *"Let the depth of your damage drown in God's plan for your life."* Even though I wrote it, reading it again hit me a little differently. As the young people would say, bars. *Wow. I just said, "As the young people would say."* I'll grace the space of maturity and move on. What that quote is saying is that no matter what you feel the damage is, it fails in comparison to what God's love and plans are for you. The damage stops breathing and no longer lives as damage in God's presence in your life. It's time to live like it. Here's an acronym to help with that: **G.R.A.C.E.**

Grow. Anytime you are presented with opportunities for growth, take them. Stagnation is an indication of expiration. You are utilizing expired tools, mindsets, or relationships past their usefulness. What you feed will grow; be mindful of what in you is being fed. Throw the expired stuff away.

Receive. Damage may make you feel like you are not worthy of receiving even God's perfect love for you. When you become a child of God, receiving is a posture because He has so much for you.

Accept. It may be a challenge to accept the gravity of things that happen. However, you give room to delusion or error if you ignore or reject what help the situation can provide.

Celebrate. Don't forget to celebrate small and big victories. You can miss out on opportunities to witness your growth by choosing not to participate in moments that can bring more joy.

Elevate. Your lowest points can be a foundation for promotion. Having the proper posture and operating inside God's will for your life are the biggest resume' builders you possess. Remember, perfection isn't a requirement for elevation.

CHAPTER

4

PERFECT FOR
THE PURSUIT

Grace Through the Beginning

In the previous chapter, we discussed some things that can stagnate growth in the beginning stages of your GraceThrough.

Now, let's talk about moving forward. Are there goals or dreams that you've been putting off, delaying, or procrastinating on? If the answer is yes, welcome to the club, but you're not welcome here. Sometimes, we're waiting for the perfect alignment of all aspects of our lives to ensure we're absolutely ready. Perhaps you've got a backup plan (Plan B for Plan A) or believe that certain things need to fall into place before you pursue. However, waiting for perfection is a surefire way just to keep waiting.

Perfection isn't a prerequisite for pursuit. Often, perfection comes as you move toward it. God's perfection can compensate for whatever you feel you lack as you go. The need for things to be aesthetically pleasing, financially bulletproof, etc., can create an illusion of perfection. True perfection, however, lies in internal and spiritual things that don't come through sheer effort alone but with faith. Faith is defined as a sure confidence in something that we can't see. You may not see the resources, people, places, or things you think you need, but through a lens of pursuit, they're there and yours for the taking. Using that same definition of faith scriptures tells us it comes by hearing the word of God. Can't see past your damage or pursuit-get the word of God in you.

GraceThrough Pursuit

Have you ever found yourself in a place where it was easier to take the route of least resistance? For example, it was easy to settle for a job because you needed money, to settle for a spouse because you were lonely, or to accept your diagnosis because you were tired of fighting. Sometimes, putting off things that are required of you costs days, weeks, months, and years of your life. Find the grace to get through your fear of failure or lack of confidence before you get lost in a sea of regret. Settling may have you wasting time that could have went toward maintaining what you did not settle for.

For years, I've wanted to start my own business, but I dedicated most of my energy and time to being an exceptional employee for others. When business opportunities did arise, I hesitated and convinced myself that I should stay behind the scenes, supporting others rather than taking the lead. I doubted that I'd receive the necessary support, and I always found myself preoccupied with other commitments, making me feel like I didn't have the time for a business.

I would engage in activities like creating logos, drafting business plans, and scheduling meetings, only to put them on hold, waiting for a better opportunity to come along. Finally, the opportunity presented itself during the pandemic, but unfortunately, the pandemic brought unexpected health challenges that nearly took my life.

Despite launching my business, I was also battling illness while trying to manage it. If I had acted on the numerous urges I received earlier, my business might have had more time to grow and develop. Now, as a result of this lesson, whenever I receive an urge, I write it down, pray about it, and move toward it. This is one way I learned to GraceThrough the beginning of things. Writing (for clarity), praying (for direction), and executing (with purpose).

GraceThrough Preparation

In your pursuits, don't underestimate preparation. There are times when you have to be prepared for whatever it is you are called to do. Preparation (not procrastination) can include acts that help create the character for your journey. It could include education, study, improved health habits, a deeper spiritual connection to God, disconnecting from sources that don't feed you, or any other active positioning. These things can also provide grace to your space of pursuit, even when things are not perfect.

Not preparing can potentially be counterproductive; it's like being a world-renowned singer who doesn't take care of their voice, an unlearned teacher, a scholar who doesn't research, a creative person who is not connected to the Creator, someone who doesn't prepare for an Olympic style race or someone not relying on God's instructions when they work for Him. Preparation shows fidelity to your pursuit. Your willingness to dedicate your efforts shows your allegiance to it, not perfection for it.

GraceThrough The Look

I understand things that impede pursuit such as stagnation, procrastination, or even depression can have a look. Some may say that outward appearance is not a factor, but I disagree, respectfully, not from a place of vanity, either. Maybe you don't have the ideal wardrobe, you're not at the ideal weight, you've experienced trauma that's left you less put together than in previous times, or you look like what you're going through. Believe me, I understand. Do you see me on the cover of this book? Had I waited to lose the weight or become an ideal size, the title of this book would have been *GraceThrough, Never.* For many of us, we have to strengthen the best parts of us while we're still improving. No matter how hard things are, there are parts of you that can still be developed. It can be your character, intellect, physique, talent, gift, or esteem. Whatever it is, don't use it to motivate you to cancel yourself before you even start.

This was a struggle I had, especially because my circumstances sometimes dictated how I presented myself. If "you look like what you've been through" was a person, it would have been me. Life was happening hard, and I had been in bed depressed for days. One day, I was craving egg salad. It was a good sign because I wasn't eating, so I left the house and went to the store for the ingredients. As I walked towards the door, I caught a glimpse of myself through the glass door. I looked so unkept, just pitiful. My clothes were wrinkled, my hair was all over the place, and I had on shoes I vowed I would never wear outside of the house.

In that moment, it was time for me to get it together. Not for a man, job, or anything, but for me. During some of my toughest moments in life I was always able to have an anointed hairdresser. As a child, I cherished those moments when my godmother styled my hair. She played a significant role in keeping my hair healthy and strong. Then, my sister took over and made sure I stayed up-to-date with the latest trends. Then there was my beloved cousin, Tiana, who is now with the Lord, who not only created unique hairstyles for me but also imparted so much in me while doing my hair. All of them provided much-needed support during difficult times. Looking good made me feel good. However, we

lived in different states at the time, and I became pro-
ficient at wearing wigs, hardly needing to visit a salon
but the way I was looking-it was time.

I had run into a stylist who I did not know personally
and remembered her when I realized it was time to at
least comb my hair. I was perfecting my wig units for my
pursuit of getting out of depression but that did nothing
for my hair underneath. I made an appointment with
her and once I arrived, I understood very quickly why
I was led to go there. My new hairstylist was able to
tackle the ugly that was being reflected on the outside
based on what was going on inside. When I first started
being serviced by her, I was so embarrassed. I asked her
to cut all my hair off and I start over because it was so
damaged, and she simply responded, "No, I'm not doing
that." What she was really saying to me was *NO, I will
not help you change your identity because you're unsure
of who you are right now.*

I would come to her with my hair that hadn't been
washed in weeks, balding spots and strands that were
tangled and matted to my head. Each time I sat in her

chair, she affirmed I had beautiful hair. Please believe she was speaking by faith because it was a mess, a cold mess because nothing hot was touching my head. Sometimes, I would cry as the water ran through my scalp. My tears and the water would meet in the sink. I was being washed inside and out.

I didn't start seeing the beauty in my hair until I showed up for several more sessions. Remember, to keep showing up. I was able to grace the space of self-care through the encouragement of my beautiful hairstylist. It was as if her care seeped into my innermost being, and I began to feel better with each visit. She prayed and sprayed and combed and groaned in the Spirit on my behalf. She had such a strong connection to God that it shed light on the connection that once mattered the most to me that I let sit in limbo long enough. There were times when my demeanor was off. I would just sit down because I was tired of crying and did not have anything to say, so I went and sat in her chair to get my hair done. Some days, she would be quiet until we went to the washroom with just her and me. As she washed my hair, she would declare healing over me and call the healed Tiana to the forefront as I sat there broken. In most appointments, she would say to me, "I wish you could see what I see, Tiana. You're going to be alright." I would sometimes think to myself, *if you say so.* I went back for months and months and kept feeling better and better. I looked forward to sharing my victories and losses with her. We grew a bond that I will forever cherish. She also helped me reconnect to my God given purpose in such a beautiful way. I felt God's presence through her and I will forever be grateful for our hair sessions and now friendship.

I began to get back to Tiana. Were things perfect? No. I was still wearing house shoes outside, but my clothes became less and less wrinkled, and people weren't telling me all the time that I looked tired after I had slept twelve hours the night before. With every step taken towards GraceThrough, I was getting better and better.

I would also go to my favorite beauty bar to ensure my eyebrows would stop connecting and watch the owner minister to others through her gift of beauty and encouragement. I saw women come in heavy, and they would leave lighter and brighter. Then, it would be my turn to sit in her chair. She always handled me so gently. I knew I would always get a good laugh, lesson, and love. I was still able to get those moments from the owner, who is my forever sister, although I was no longer married to her brother. Talk about GraceThrough. There was no way to properly prepare for these types of moments. However, I had to be present to experience the beauty in them. While they helped to get me together, on the outside, God was and still is orchestrating this beautiful, spiritual journey that I would not trade for anything. It may sound vain to some, but fixing your outer appearance can reflect your spirit man is being taken care of.

In those moments, I obtained strength that, although I was not perfect, there were things I still needed to pursue, even in my pain. It's not just about the aesthetic. However, it helped. To anyone in the beauty service industry, you have the ability to engage with people during some of their most vulnerable times. More than likely, you are aware that you have a special gift to connect with people and provide comfort. Please never take

for granted that God has trusted you with helping people on their journey. You may be used to help someone
understand they don't have to be perfect or polished,
just pushed. You may be that push of confidence they
need to go to higher heights and deeper depths. Your
services may be the encouragement someone needs not
to give up. May God bless you on your journey!

GraceThrough What You Feel

Maybe it's not a problem with how you look. It may be
a problem with how you feel. You may be struggling
with understanding your worth or too busy comparing
other people's journeys with your own. Whatever you're
feeling, it does not disqualify you from receiving and
pursuing what belongs to you. There's not much in life
that you will face that will be wasted and that can't be
used to strengthen your current journey or encourage
someone else on theirs. What have you been preparing
but have not acted on? Maybe it's your own book or a
business idea. Maybe it's finally prioritizing your relationship with God. Maybe it's spreading the gospel of

Jesus Christ in the way He has instructed you. Whatever it may be, do your best to grace the space of pursuit! If not, you leave the spaces you're meant to grace up for grabs to be occupied by another.

GraceThrough Isolation

How often do you isolate yourself and stop being present when you are going through difficult times rather than creating healthy boundaries? It's in those moments you convince yourself that you are not a "people person," "I can do bad all by myself," or my all-time favorite, "I'm in a season of isolation." There may be some traces of validity in those statements; however, if you don't show up, how will you receive what it is you need? Spaces of difficulty require you, too. I understand that you need time alone at times. However, living a life that does not include shared spaces with other people can cause your senses to become dull to what can sharpen you. Don't hide longer than needed, or some spaces will be removed when you're not there to grace them.

5

SENSE THE OFFENSE
Grace Through Offense

Now that we've discussed the concept of GraceThrough, it's essential to consider factors or behaviors that disrupt your GraceThrough and hinder your ability to extend grace to others or your personal journey. Here are a few examples:

- Hidden insecurities: they can develop into jealousy and envy.

- Struggling with forgiveness. How can you expect to be forgiven if you don't forgive? You may have an even bigger problem on your hands.
- Issues with your identity. How can you not fall victim to the labels this world can place on you if you don't know who you are?
- Abandonment or rejection. They can cause you to be hyper-accepting of things you should reject or accepting of things that are not good for you.
- A hardened heart because of displaced pain and anger.

One of the many GraceThrough destroyers that stick out more than the others is offense. In a conversation I was having with someone, they felt compelled to say that because of my weight, I had a slim chance of becoming a CEO of anyone's company. Maybe they had a valid point. After all, there are risks associated with being overweight. However, the biggest risk in the conversation was attempting to shame someone who is not ashamed. That moment could have been an ideal breeding ground for offense to grow. It had all the essentials: seeds of doubt, insecurity, and some good unresolved trauma water. Here's the thing: I didn't subscribe to it, so the offense was no good. While the opinion may have been valid for them, I couldn't yoke my identity to that level of thought. As it relates to offense, whether intentionally directed to you or not, resist living a life that attracts or receives offense. I've since GracedThrough to become the CEO of my own company. It's big too, bigger than me. (Pun intended)

People who feel offended often let it influence them, making them perceive offense more strongly than it really is. Have you met someone who easily gets offended by small things? Here's a more important question: are you that person? Offense acts like a thief. It steals your peace, distorts your perspective, and hinders your progress. It's crucial to prioritize your peace over seeking revenge or dwelling on the emotions tied to being offended. Your perspective gets twisted when you see things through the lens of offense. In short, you can't grace the space of offense because offense is your offender.

Now, if you feel offended by the truth or something that helps you grow, there's another issue to consider. Imagine being in a dark room, when light is introduced, your initial reaction is usually to close your eyes or shield your face. However, as the light expands, you become more comfortable in it. Similarly, if someone points out that your life is in disarray (light) and suggests solutions, you might feel offended or even attacked. Instead, let that offense prompt you to tidy up your life once the light has been shining on it for a while. Sometimes, the pain of a situation highlights areas for improvement, leading to our GraceThrough. Let the light shine.

We won't be addressing the kind of offense that arises when confronted with what you need. The offense I'm referencing is the offense that permits you to be offended just for the sake of being able to. The type of offense that stems from pain, trauma, hurt feelings, miscommunication, and even jealousy.

Yes, offense can come from jealousy. You may be offended that someone had the courage to do something you were supposed to do, and rather than being inspired, you compare yourself in a way to discredit their progress. You know, things we say like "That little business," or "It must be nice," or even "If that were me." Well, it's not you, and your offense to their success may be a reason you have not experienced GraceThrough in that area. I will share a key to life if you have this struggle. Learn to celebrate with others; I mean genuinely feel happy for others' success, even if you can't label or define it. What God has for you is for you, AND what He has for someone else is for them, too. Drop out of the comparison race. You will never win.

For years, I was offended by a certain demographic, all of them. My skin would crawl, and I would be super uncomfortable and defensive when we had to occupy the same space. I tried to avoid them, but it was inevitable. So what I did was warn every one of my feelings (spreading offense) so they wouldn't be caught off guard if I came out of character around them. Depending on who I told and how I felt, if you didn't agree with me or challenged my perspective (accountability), you became an opp. (That means opponent for those who didn't know either.) All my feelings actually came from a place in my childhood that I never let go of.

One day, I was playing outside with my siblings and neighborhood kids. While my back was turned to the street, someone driving by threw an ear of corn at my back and sped off while screaming, "Nigger!" The offense took root from that day and grew and took on a life of its own. My best friend at the time was Caucasian, but I wasn't racist (I'll digress) and even began to look at her and her family differently. I had a hard time engaging with people who did not look like me. Eventually, I faced the contradiction of claiming to love my neighbor only if I could tolerate their race. God helped me recognize my mistake and infused me with the grace to give and receive love to everyone I encountered, authentically. What I learned was I, the church girl, had severe anger inside of me. Learning that helped me to identify the real offense. The product of my built-up anger.

Excessive offense is a matter of you believing you have the right to be uncomfortable with someone's existence at that moment. Harsh truth: as that therapist told me, whether it's intentional or not, the offense is your responsibility to heal and get over. This could mean removing yourself from the situation, creating boundaries, and even repenting for decisions you made by sticking around too long. This mindset has to settle in your innermost being, including your body, or even your body will suffer because of the offense.

In 2021, I was sick and near death. I was found on the bathroom floor and woke up in the Intensive Care Unit (ICU). The conditions leading up to the sickness included hidden trauma, resentment, anger, and poor spiritual health. The truth was, I was really tired. I had been fighting to keep my marriage, fighting to keep my sanity, fighting to find my purpose amid life changes, and now I had to fight for my life. During the fight, the offense had settled in. I was offended by the rejection and abandonment that I was feeling. So, anything that resembled those feelings became my punching bag.

Being exposed to an illness that was designed to prosper in my impaired conditions did not make things any better. It was as if the sickness could smell the blood of my offense and attacked in full force. (Some of you are bleeding, and the aroma of the offense has become a trail to find you. You've left traces that have become a road map for whatever is after you.) After being released from the ICU, I was left on my back for months, unable to walk or care for myself completely. I was grateful to be home but now offended that I even got sick. Eventually, GraceThrough kicked in.

During that time, I had no distractions. I was too weak to pick up my phone for long periods, so I had little social media influence. I couldn't even shop over it. In my confused state, I tried to order something online and sent the items to an address that was not mine. I could not church it away because I couldn't get to the building. I couldn't socialize through it, think through it, or allow my charity for others to justify my lack of self-accountability. At some point, it felt like the physical ailments were getting worse. I had to turn my attention to my spiritual self.

The healing journey was so ugly and embarrassing at times, especially because I depended on someone else to take care of me physically. In hindsight, even that worked for my good because I would have created a super independent version of myself as a means to not deal with what was eating at me. Often, as women, our desire to do things ourselves is an offensive posture against those who dropped the ball in our lives. In this instance, I had no choice but to depend on someone else.

I remember asking my mother-in-law at the time (who is still my mother after the divorce) as I laid on my back sobbing on a tear-soaked pillow, "Why is this happening to me?" and I kept repeating, "Why me?" She simply said, "Tiana, you will get through this." She was absolutely right.

At some point, all my energy went into addressing the offense whether I wanted to or not. The sickness was secondary to the issues of my heart and mind. While I found the resolve to get through and GraceThrough, it doesn't always take hardships, challenges, or even sickness to reach the state of GraceThrough. It could be forgiving yourself or others for what you did not know or handle properly.

Maybe you're having a hard time accepting that it's an offense that's hurting you and not your imaginary haters. Maybe you believe you're hiding it? Nope, it's showing. You feel the weight of it at the most inopportune times because it's in you and impacting your movements. Offense is designed to distort things. Even the purest intent of others can look like a personal attack to someone operating in offense.

Offense has a way of attaching itself to your being, which impacts the way that you hear, smell, taste, see, and touch. Think about a time you allowed offense or a grudge to settle in you. Remember it? Now, think of how even your body perceived the offense. You say things like, "That smell reminds me of...", "I can't even look at..." Or you overcompensate with nice gestures to prove it's not really there. How much more money, time, and energy will you spend to prove that you are not offended by something that clearly bothers you? It's time to GraceThrough it fully and place some healthy boundaries while you're at it.

Let's test your senses for offense. Think about the following as you ensure offense does not take root in any of your senses. Consider these questions as you rid your senses of any offense that is impairing your ability to GraceThrough.

- **See:** Are you seeing anything through a lens that contains streaks of offense? Do you only see yourself?

- **Taste:** Is the fruit of your mouth sweet, sour, or nasty? If what comes out of your mouth is foul, check your heart. It's not just "you." It's something that is hurting you. What if you had to eat your own words? How would they taste?

- **Hear:** What are you perceiving that is coming through your ear gate? How do compliments sound? What about critique? If everything sounds the same, listen for offense - it's loud for everyone else. You will eventually hear it if it's there.

- **Smell:** Are there certain things that trigger your smell? A lotion, cologne, or reminder of an unpleasant situation? Are you avoiding anything that may be good for you because of its smell?
- **Touch:** Are there things that you shouldn't touch or feel, but your offense justifies it? Is your offense causing you to isolate yourself?

If you can sense the offense, others can, too. Offense does not have to be the loudest voice in the room. Nor does it have to be your life's narrative.

6

VOICEOVER

Grace Through the Narrators

Have you ever seen pictures or a video with a voice narrating over the muted visuals? That's called a voiceover. Likely used for storytelling, humor, or drama, it explains what's happening or what will happen with the voice as the main narrating tool. Similarly, God's word has spoken about you to the world's audience. Just as a voiceover evokes emotions to keep the audience engaged, consider if the voice you are allowing to speak over you is God's voice or another. Please consider that question as you keep reading. Sometimes, the voice and visuals may not perfectly align, but they always work together. Is that what your visuals portray?

My mother often shares the story that at two years old, she moved into a new apartment and instructed me to stand in a corner out of the way while the movers were working. She said she unpacked and was going to start cooking and went to look for me because she had not heard from me, and over an hour later, I was still waiting on the wall that she had asked me to while the movers were busy. She spoke, and I listened even as a small child. I did not move until she told me to. There were other times in life when I waited on others to tell me what to do before I moved. I listened to instructions. Unfortunately, if wisdom was not the loudest voice, I may not have listened.

In our home growing up, I was the oldest. I was a parentified child and took my role as the house manager seriously. My parents always told us to look out for one another, and one way I listened to their voices, was making sure we went to church. If that wasn't looking out for them, I did not know what was because for me, church was it. I became the one who convinced all my siblings to come to church every week. I would get up and make sure we were all ready, hopefully for my favorite, which was Sunday School. Then, I would get home to make sure my schoolwork was completed for the next day.

I also excelled as a student, especially when taking tests. I was being shaped to respect the voices of those who provided my identity. My parents, leaders at church and especially my teachers. After I understood the voice of the teacher administering tests, I knew how to prepare for them. I knew that I needed to study only the text-book for some teachers because they rarely deviated from it. I also knew at times; I would need notes from the teachers themselves if it were a teacher who was passionate about the subject. I often obtained those notes, too. If I knew there would be bonus questions, I would always ask leading questions to get an idea of what the teacher was looking for. A voice often acti-vated my actions because I listened very well. What I heard often presented through my actions because, again, I wasn't sure who I was until you told me. It was almost like I was a voice-activated robot waiting for the next voice for my instruction. The biggest problem with living like that, looking back was God's voice was the faintest in my life at times, even though I was a church girl.

As a teenager I tried to listen to the voice that said I needed to fit in. I faced legal issues as a teenager for not only hitting a parked car after only driving eight seconds down the street with no license but for also presenting an ID to the officer that I used the night before at a night club. Let me mention the club scene was not what it was cracked up to be especially because I would zone out and start singing gospel songs in my head. That's what happens when the voiceover does not match the picture-no alignment. When the courts asked for character references from school officials, I was so embarrassed. Many of them assumed I was going through something traumatic in life that made me do it because it was so out of character for me. Nope, just listening to the wrong voice. How confusing for an A+ student, church girl to have legal issues because she wanted to go to a night club and sing gospel songs and then crash her friend's car and use someone else's ID in one weekend. Whatever voice I was listening to eventually switched, thankfully. I was confused just writing that narrative so I can only imagine if I continued to live it out.

Define vs. Describe

I found much of my identity through the descriptions of me in my going to church without a real relationship with God days. I was told I was dramatic and always involved in something, making me believe at times that God was not with me if I needed to express myself, so I would just shut up. When others had issues with me, I would become hyper-accommodating, thinking I was taking the high road- even if it was an attack from hell. I was told I could not sing, and although they were right to a certain extent, I never knew what to do with my love for music, so I suppressed it. I was told I was good at things that surrounded learning and education, and so I never sought anything outside of that realm. I learned the Lake of Fire was a place I genuinely wanted to avoid (and still do). I was taught that God detests sin and that we would face consequences for our wrongdoings. So, that voice led me to live in fear of consequences. The fear sometimes crippled me from actually living. Not only that but there were times that I rejected God's grace because it did not sound like the voice I had made God to be through others I had listened to. Real GraceThrough is learning God and His voice for yourself.

As a young adult, I fell and broke my leg and ankle. Fellow churchgoers, whose opinions I valued, questioned me, and implied the injury was a result of something wrong I had done, and I believed them. I convinced myself that I deserved the injury, and I would have to deal with the impact of it forever, and maybe that would lessen the chance that I would be in trouble with God.

Now, please understand I don't blame the "church" for anything. People who have experienced the most "church hurt" are those who have faithfully served, so please don't take this as a church-bashing moment. I don't align with those principles, and neither should you. My point is that I, at some point in my walk with God, allowed the voice of people to overpower the voice of God. Yes, leaders can lead you to themselves more than they do to Christ. However, we must take responsibility if we follow them there. Before we blame another institution, person, or climate for the state of our we should ask, "Who am I listening to? "and "What voice am I allowing to guide my life?' Consider this: whatever you respond to, has your ear.

One night, my cousins called me to go to church. I put my big black boot on my broken leg and ankle and made it to church. I put on a long skirt that swept the ground so no one would be able to see my boot because it was not cute at all. It was a spirit-filled service, and I really was enjoying it, but my leg was throbbing! I wanted to elevate it but did not want to bring attention to myself, so I sat and took the pain because I left my meds at home and did not take them before I left. As I sat down and began to mentally check out of the service to focus on the pain, the guest preacher did an altar call. This one was different than any other I had seen or experienced. She began to mention situations, and if they applied to you, you were asked to come up for prayer. I was so encouraged by what I was witnessing it brought me to tears. Based on some of the things she mentioned, there was no way she would have known, especially because she lived hundreds of miles away. It was so beautiful to see everyone so blessed by experiencing God in that way.

Then, she said there was someone there struggling with a broken or painful left leg and ankle. Those who knew looked at me, and I looked away. Her voice was good for the others, but that was not the voice I was tuned into at that time, because I was so focused on the pain. After some pushing, I snapped out of my focus and went up to the altar. As I approached her, she reached out her hand to pray and I pulled up my skirt for her to see the cast and boot, and the rest was history. As she prayed over me, the love of God showered me- that feeling was familiar from when I was younger. I remember feeling like I was being hugged. Everyone in the building rejoiced with me, and in the presence of the Lord, I wept and felt sadness leave my body. Yes, she prayed for my leg, but my spirit was rejuvenated, and that overpowered everything I went up for. I walked away from the altar, filled with so much joy. As I walked, I remember thinking to myself that I needed to position myself a certain way to walk so that I would not fall or be in too much more pain. But, as I continued to walk, I noticed there was no pain! I began to run in my big black boot. Then, I heard a voice that said take it off. I did just that. I experienced a miracle that night, and God's voice was re-established over my life. What I loved about this voiceover was the picture of my life was positioning toward what God said.

That moment was not an isolated incident for me. I had been sick before, and the same power that healed me before, healed me again. Reading another letter that I wrote to myself showed me that God was always speaking healing whether I heard Him or not. When I was sick and secluded in that room earlier in the book, I began hearing the voice of God like never before. I can see it in this letter excerpt:

"Never forget that if He did it before....you know the rest. Tiana, I know you wonder if you will ever make it out of this room. I just want you to know that I am proud of you. After all that you have been through, you're still here and fighting. Don't ever give up. God has you just like He always has. Now put this away and practice your breathing."

I did, in fact, make it out of that room and have since entered rooms of health and wealth because God told me that I would. The next year, following being sick, I received a promotion (almost doubling my salary), the car that I was going to gift myself in a few years, and a beautiful place to call my own. These are all things I was believing God for before I became sick. The sickness did not stop God's voice over me. None of the situations I faced did either. Let this serve as a re-established resolve to seek and hear God louder than anything or anyone.

In those times, when you feel voiceless or unheard, you may permit others to label you even when you're not labeling yourself. I heard a very powerful quote in a service one day. He said, "If they can't define you, they will describe you." I don't know exactly who they were, but I knew exactly what he was referring to. In those moments of quietness, you sometimes allow others the opportunity to define you based on some of your attributes. If I'm acting like damaged goods, even when I'm trying to break free from the label, I may be treated like damaged goods. If I'm acting desperate, I may be treated as if I am desperate. If my behavior suggests that I have low self-esteem, I may be treated as such.

For me, it was something like this: if my behavior were dramatic, I would be shunned or uninvited to certain spaces because I was full of drama. The truth of the matter is my personality is that of order and confrontation with things that disrupt order. But if you describe me without knowing who I really am, you'll label me improperly. Some of us have labeled people based on a description of their behavior rather than understanding who they are. Who they are may annoy you because they are called to confront what's inside of you. Don't be so quick to use your description of even yourself to define who God says you are if it does not confirm what God has said concerning you.

The voiceover also speaks to the voice(s) you are allowing in and through your senses. Be it in person or on social media; you rarely realize how easily things can seep into your life and influence how you operate just because of what you listen to or watch. What you are allowing in your ear and eye gates matters. If it didn't, you wouldn't be presented with so many images and voices.

At times, you may not even feel captivated by your own story. Maybe you've checked out or just been silent. Even in hiding, you're still on display. The thing about this voiceover is your story is being watched through others hearing and seeing the voice of God over your life. As you're moving through, He's speaking life into you through His word, and it's enticing others to watch! Your GraceThrough is giving others a chance to hear and see God's promises fulfilled through you. Even your adversary will get the picture.

If you're ever in a place of uncertainty in your life, the voice you are listening to becomes paramount. If you're experiencing any type of identity crisis or prolonged transition, you're a prime target for voiceovers that speak to your insecurities. We could really unpack the position of the voices in your life, but for the sake of GraceThrough, we can unpack some of the voices I have allowed to define my life at times.

Not everything will stick, but if you're not careful, it will. In the upcoming paragraphs are some things that I heard much of my life. Many of them seemed complimentary. Hearing these things became so consistent that I took it on as my truth, even if it was not. Pay attention to what's being said, especially when you're no longer gracing that space. It's okay for people to describe you as good, bad, or indifferent. It doesn't have to define you. I always try to consider what God said about me before I become accommodating of others' opinions, even if they are valid. I am called to engage with people. Even when I am in periods of isolation, God is down-loading strategies and wisdom to me concerning others. Not being around people for long periods has not been an option for me for much of my life. It took me a while to even consider not accepting everything said to me especially in times I made mistakes or missed the mark. However, what God has said trumps anything else I listened to or considered. Rather than giving weight to isolation, offense, and annoyance, I've learned to put voices in their proper places by labeling the label, so it peels off me. Here are some examples of what I've heard and had to put in its proper place.

You're cute in the face. All of me is beautiful; God made me. Just because you can't accept my bigness in mind, body, and spirit as a beauty standard does not mean you can exclude the rest of me. You're cute, too!

I feel sorry for you. Please don't. There are other things you should feel in life. Sorry for me is not one of them. Even this conversation is working for my good. Sometimes, pity serves as a standard for those who don't really value you.

I'm so comfortable around you. Don't get too comfortable because as soon as I challenge you or you are offended, I won't be so easy to be around. Comfort does not mean compliance or even connection. I am happy you can enjoy my space, though.

You're too judgmental. If you feel that way, that's fine. There are some things that I won't tolerate in my space, and you shouldn't tolerate in yours. Don't forget judgement from someone qualified to judge, can vindicate you or help you see what you need to fix.

You're so quiet. I learned to speak when needed. I can be a chatterbox when I'm engaged in something of interest, or my words are required. It's wisdom and not a lack of ability.

You're really nice. I try to be, but that doesn't mean you can treat me any kind of way. Nor does it mean I have to tolerate abuse, neglect, or demonic activity, thank you.

You're really mean. Is it because you can no longer benefit from the naivety I possessed when I was overly accommodating?

You have a mean face, but you're actually cool when I get to know you. You judged me by what you perceived, and you were wrong. Nice to meet you, too.

I highly recommend taking some time for self-reflection on the labels or identities given to you or those you've adopted. Have you accepted an identity given to you by others? Dig deeper to understand its true significance and ensure it aligns with who God has called you to be. This is at the core of GraceThrough: living with the awareness that, thanks to your connection with Christ Jesus, you're more than a conqueror. Regardless of life's challenges, you can gain wisdom and navigate with grace, in grace, and through grace. Without God's voice, the pictures in your voiceover just don't make sense. Make sure to embrace the space of God's voice, here's another acronym to help, **V.O.I.C.E:**

Vindication - God's truth will free you from false narratives without your exertion. The lie will die.

Omniscience - Wherever you're heading, God has already been there.

Intellect - God intentionally and clearly placed you here. No need to feel overwhelmed. He was intentional with you, be the same with Him.

Choice - You're still here, you hold value, and you're God's chosen occupant of space and time in this world. There is nothing anyone can say, do, or feel that can change that. YOU ARE GOD'S CHOICE!

Expression - You are one of God's children, revealing aspects of God's nature to those who seek to know. Confuse the enemy, not those who seek to understand God.

Your GraceThrough, space, pursuit, offense, damage, and voices truly begin with your relationship with Jesus. Salvation through Him is the ultimate grace. In simple terms, GraceThrough is inseparable from the Giver of Grace! We need rescue from ourselves and the lack of connection to the One who spoke us into existence. Reflecting on my experiences, much remains untold in this book. Left to my own devices, I can only imagine where I would be. Offenses would have worsened my condition, the struggle to understand myself would have deepened confusion, and the lack of wisdom would have ensured I would remain bound. Once again, I hope something in this book will inspire and even cause a call to action. Since our journeys have crossed paths through this book, let's GraceThrough, Again.

GRACETHROUGH LETTER

Hallelujah! I offer my heartfelt gratitude to God for guiding me through this journey. I want to express my thanks to all those who have been sources of inspiration and support in my life. To my mother, who gave me my first push into this world, and for all the pushes ever since, I love you! To my other mother, Ms. Mary, you have been a constant source of encouragement since 2015. To my godmother, thank you for your unwavering love. To my grandmother, Betty Petty, your resounding "Yes" to God continues to propel me forward.

Pastor Christina, your guidance will forever hold a special place in my heart. Ms. Pat, thank you for looking out for me! Tiana, I miss you deeply, and I know you would be one of my most fervent cheerleaders right now. Rest well.

*To the Hooks clan, my first and forever besties - my siblings and their little ones, I carry you with me wherever I go. Let's not forget Tia and all of my beloved cousins, relatives, and **all** of my aunties - I cherish each and every one of you. To my dad Woody, I love you.*

I want to give special thanks to W.O.G.I.T., my very first ministry endeavor. You have provided me a space of grace, and I believe that God has even greater plans in store for us.

To those I've had the privilege of calling a friend, I have an immense love for you - and there's nothing you can do about it. You have been a constant reminder that God's love CAN be displayed through that of a friend. A special shout-out to Sharelle, Sheba, and Audrey. Thank y'all.

To Dr. Jeremiah Daniel Davis and my Teach Me family, we're doing it here and now!

To all the connections I've made in life so far at various spaces in my life, that pushed me to GraceThrough including (but not limited to) Ms. Sheila, Jerome, Chad,

Desmond, Apostle Sheba Brown, Pam, Amy, Chef Tae, the Sanders family, the Sheldon family, and the BGCNEO team, I want to emphasize my appreciation. Let's continue to grace every space meant for us!

With so much love,

Tiana

www.ingramcontent.com/pod-product-compliance
Lightning Source LLC
Chambersburg PA
CBHW060342130626
46553CB00003B/1082